Splashing Pink

A Poetic Conversation

by

Annie Cowell & Sam Szanto

First published 2023 by The Hedgehog Poetry Press,

5 Coppack House, Churchill Avenue, Clevedon. BS21 6QW

www.hedgehogpress.co.uk

Copyright © Annie Cowell & Sam Szanto 2023

The right of Annie Cowell & Sam Szanto to be identified as the authors of this work has been asserted in accordance with the Copyright, Designs and Patents Act 1988. All rights reserved. No part of this publication may be reproduced, stored in or introduced into a retrieval system, or transmitted in any form, or by any means (electronic, mechanical, photocopying, recording or otherwise) without prior written permissions of the publisher. Any person who does any unauthorised act in relation to this publication may be liable for criminal prosecution and civil claims for damages.

ISBN: 978-1-913499-98-3

"*Splashing Pink* is a conversation between two mothers from two different generations. It is a series of poems in which the nature of motherhood is explored; from the early days following birth to the experience of watching your child becoming a parent themselves. It delves into questions about what it means to be a mother, what they will do for their children and how even mother nature strives to create harmony, ease pain and 'splash pink' on lives."

This book is dedicated to Annie's children, Jessica and Jonathan, and Sam's children, Rufus and Iris.

Contents

Night-light 7
My son wears his fear 8
The Sun Rises 9
Skin 10
Looking Back 11
First Day for Liz 12
First Day of Term 13
Swaddled 14
Untethering 15
The Eagle Nights 16
Early Morning 17
Brambling 18
Empty Nest 19
Sunday lunch rituals began on Saturday 20
A Trail of Two Cities 21
When the sun fell out of the sky 22

The dialogue begins with 'Night-light' by Sam Szanto then continues alternately.

NIGHT-LIGHT

In the night-light, I watch your eyelashes
lengthen. You snuffle and squeak as you
feed, my little pig. You soberly suck,
my small life locked into your rosebud lips.

You are my first responsibility,
a watery sun I revolve around;
I teeter on the edges of my self,
moon-tide milk flowing from my bruised body.

Life ended and started when you began,
pushed out from under my skin, but still in;
we're marooned together in the soft dark,
your eating imperative, half-violent.

As I tiptoe with you to your basket,
a bird's yellow song creeps into the room
tangling with your sounds: mewls, snores, grunts, snarfles;
then quick, sharp breaths as you roam dream country.

Some unknown evil makes you wake and wail.
I swoop. Your appalled mouth is a door shoved
open, cries spilling out, echoing through
time. Every mother runs to that red sound.

I breast-bury your sad-indignant vowels,
the night growing around us. Days tighten.
We are in limbo, suspended between
lives, waiting for the people we will be.

I still expect you to vanish at night,
my refugee, so new to this country.
The fact of you is thin and silvery,
but you're more important to me than me.

MY SON WEARS HIS FEAR

like a thick winter coat he can't take off.
I would love to undo the buttons
and remove it for him.
But this is not a fluttery fear
to be trapped moth-like under glass,
released through a window,
it is not a monster under his bed
vanquished by the flick of a light switch.
This man child of mine is a father now
with fears as new as his baby.
Born too soon,
his son was wired and tubed
for weeks inside a plastic womb.
My child wears his fears as creases
around his eyes, crumpled as his unmade bed.
I long to smooth the lines, to hold him close,
to tell him not to worry.
But he is a world away
so I do not wear *my* fears. They hang
behind a door of polished words
and reassuring smiles.
Only at night, when the only lights
are celestial bodies
do I pull the robes of fear around me.

THE SUN RISES

Your snarfles unsealing sleep from my eyes
I rise, heart sinking at the hour, and stand
at your door, watching you beached in your cot,
blank-faced as a clock, but then you see me,

a smile stretching your skin, my face
shining through yours, and you ascend,
a wobbly king, hands clutching bars,
jabbering about cars, enchanted at being awake,

thrilling to be living on a Monday so large.
Though I feel trodden on as a carpet
I love this time of love at the edges
of the blinds, when cheek to cheek

we watch amaranth melt into child's-hair gold,
I point out a fox slinking on the street,
recycling bins lined up so very neat,
the unromantic stuff of our kingdom.

The sun rises and I shape you to me.

SKIN

Birth gave you a strawberry;
its succulent crimson
fading now -

a shadow as faint as

that white line on your knee;
  a
    fall
       in the park.
The knuckle you sliced
with an army knife.
A patch on your back
which itches when
the seasons change.

Your skin, my son,
I know it like my own.

LOOKING BACK

When my son was in Year Two I moved him
from almost everything he knew
to a city which had been a holiday, a school
neither of us had been to
before we climbed the steep hill that April Monday,
I pointed out a board: posters advertising
holiday clubs, a bake sale, an Easter bunny hunt,
That's the past, he said, face fresh-page blank and white.
We stood, an island of silence in the playground,
hands interlocked like the Duplo blocks we used to play with
on days at home that I thought would never end.
Filled to the margins with worry, I held his clammy hand,
his other wobbling the tooth that hung by a thread,
children moving around us: fighting screeching laughing.
Finally a woman with a lanyard marched
from a redbrick building, on hearing my son was new
her face flowered open and she crouched to speak to him,
ushering him away as my heart disappeared
in quicksand, *Love you*, I called, hand held in a wave
that was also a stop sign, he looked back once
and then was gone. I lingered on,
a neon-jacketed Breakfast Club Noah's Ark-ing past,
women with double buggies, clusters of chatting mothers,
before drifting away like white-grey cloud from the sun.

Three years on, my son will only hold my hand
to cross a road, and never looks back
when he goes into school.
                                            I do.

FIRST DAY FOR LIZ

In an overcast Scottish sky, a plane circles
like a call on hold, carrying a lady in waiting.
Below, at Balmoral, the self-proclaimed
booster rocket splashes out.
It is unlikely we will see photos
of him ploughing. A chorus of low thunder
fills the short interval before the Queen
offers her hand for the fifteenth time.
The kiss is symbolic.
Instead a small handshake suffices
to greet the latest Prime Minster.
She bears the same moniker, but
unlike Elizabeth, *she* uses the diminutive.
Liz.
Liz promises to deliver a better future,
to be like Hera, protector of children.
Tonight, as she closes her door
on this first day of her government
will she, as mother, hold her breath and listen
for noises in the street?
Or will she simply kiss her children
good night and toddle off to bed?

FIRST DAY OF TERM

Autumn has slipped in, children at school again
twenty-nine in Year Five in one Mersey primary,
trying to think of what to say, their teacher lay awake
for a week, nothing came, there is no lesson to learn,
no way to splash pink on the pain,
at assembly the headteacher's calm cliches
are delivered to restless uncertain faces
and there is counselling for the classmates
sobbing ceaselessly

at Olivia's bedroom window, her mother stands
watching the kids walk home, hands clutched
tight by their parents, faces known for years
and barely known at all, they frequently glance
at the door, slow neck twists bringing the glances back,
they don't see the woman there, mummified in grief,
they see a gunman, a burglar, police,
blood blood blood, sepia television scenes,

I gaze at the beaming girl on screen, read the headlines'
broken piano noise before putting my phone away
to fetch my children, the six-year-old runs towards me
and into my arms, the nine-year-old is quieter, cooler,
when he's out of the playground he skips
in time to the glowing notes in his head,
he's further from me everyday, but still
here, still mine.

SWADDLED

I call my son.
When he answers I see that he is walking
in the park. Before he speaks he unzips
his coat a little, exposing the closed eye
and soft cheek of my grandson
who is swaddled there.
Wouldn't he be safer in his buggy?
The words jump out like hiccups.
Last time, when we were speaking like this
a rogue cyclist almost collided with him.

My son cocks an eyebrow but pauses
nonetheless, sits on a bench under a tree.
My shoulders lower a little. As we chat
I reel in the invisible cord which binds us.
Light ripples in the green pool of shade
where we paddle together for a while
before clouds gather and he stands,
ready to leave.
I begin to utter more words of caution,
but my son, as ever, is two steps ahead.
Keeping the cord taut between us
he zips his jacket up higher.
He's safe beside me.
He can listen to my heartbeat.

UNTETHERING

At the door, the four untether
from their mothers,
Luca jumps up and down,
Iris shows her plaster collection,
Anaya is crying,
Isabelle goes silent,

their mothers retreat to a cafe
saying how free they feel
and talking only of their children,
Isabelle's reading fluently,
Luca is being assessed for ADHD,
Anaya's no longer dry at night,
Iris is jealous of the new baby,

stick-like limbs held in a polyester embrace
the four find their places at round tables,
staring at other kids claiming the classroom,
smiley Miss Connor gives out name stickers
and asks questions about families, pets, holidays,
'Isabelle's not talking', Iris says helpfully,
'my baby sister doesn't either, look
at my biggest plaster.'
Anaya is still crying,
Luca knocks a pot of pencils over,

at three fifteen they file out,
burgundy bags thumping their knees
they scud across the asphalt,
clammy fingers dig deep for treats,
they ignore interrogations about lunch,
playtime, new friends,
Anaya's eyes are dry,
Iris says she helped a girl find the end
of the sticky tape and gave Luca a plaster,
Isabelle's mum asks if she enjoyed herself
and did she talk to her teacher?
Mouth stuck with sweets, her daughter shrugs.

THE EAGLE NIGHTS

An eagle got trapped in my daughter's
dreams when she was small.
Each night it flew through her closed window,
stubbornly stuck in its wonky frame
and beat its wings against the walls of her room.
It flapped in a furious frenzy
of yellow eyes talons and beak, hurling
itself against the glass.

Once, as my daughter struggled
to escape in sleep, she ran from her room
and tumbled down the stairs.
Her cries tugged me to where she lay,
like a crumpled tissue of snot and tears
her arms still balled around her head,
imagining the bird would come.
Safe in my arms I soothed and smoothed
until her sobbing stopped.

Back upstairs, I pulled and pulled
fighting layers of paint and gravity
until at last, with a blast of cold
night air, the window moved. It opened,
yawning into the beetle blackness
of the small hours and together
we freed the eagle.
Watched it fly away.

EARLY MORNING

and I'm dreaming the era before kids
painted on my bones

    rupture

always at six thirty, my six-year-old Judgement, talking talking talking... Odd Socks Day today, a merit mark yesterday, and Mollie was mean, and big chips and sweetcorn, and chocolate pie and ice-cream...

    Cobwebs of sleep clinging,

    I struggle

    up, hooked fish,

Did you dream last night?

    I don't dream.

Her body duvets me, briefly,
the curtains

    wrench, a daily hunt for 'sunset',

and there it is, the pink of her ear muffs, in the east.

I would never have seen it.

BRAMBLING

Bramble bushes tangle along the railway line
near our house like clumps of unbrushed hair.
All summer, insects tend to flowery garlands, until,
come September, a jewelled coronet
lures us to the dense barbs.
After school, we scoot the track, scale the fence
onto the narrow path beside the line. Clattering
with buckets we scour amongst bullets
of green and red, hunting for ripe black garnets.
We loot from the outside in,
plundering berries the birds have missed,
cramming our mouths with greedy fistfuls.
Dark drupelets are defenceless behind leaves;
an army of spikes useless against
foraging fingers. We delve deep
into musty hearts, brushing aside cobwebs
and fat moths, wings too gluey with seeds
and juice to flutter far.
Time runs away in the lengthening
shadows; until at last we notice the first pinch
of an autumn dusk and stagger home
scratched and bloodied with purple.

Our childhoods were in those bramble buckets.
Mam cooked it into pies and crumbles,
jammed and jarred it into memories
we could preserve forever.

EMPTY NEST

Suddenly they were close again
as the two syllables of their name,
absorbed by big-small lockdown dramas,
a blackbird ferrying fluff and sticks to a hedge in March
and beakfuls of worms in April,
in those long days of a never-before-seen colour
a cat's-cradle of care threaded around the fingers
of both, controlled by one and then passed
to the other,

now the mother is on unfamiliar A roads
in muted autumn light, the sun taking final breaths,
the car stuffed with her girl's life, bigger
than she thought possible, beside her, her girl
tapping and scrolling, refusing to chat
and unwilling to stop, even for her favourite
vanilla latte,

in the car park the mother circles to find a space,
they lug in bags and boxes, dump them
on hard carpet, she holds her daughter
as long as possible, heart bruised
in the shape of a wing. Reversing carefully
to avoid new arrivals she misses her daughter,
small light on, looking out of the window
trying to see her.

SUNDAY LUNCH RITUALS BEGAN ON SATURDAY

with a bag of veg Dad brought
from his allotment. It was a lucky dip
of corkscrew carrots, spuds like hearts
and asteroids, huge heads of cabbage.
Before bed Mam would place dried peas,
hard as ball bearings, in a cold bath to soak;
by Sunday morning, when Karen Carpenter's
vinyl voice crooned from the living room,
they would've relaxed a little, be ready
for a slow stew to green mush.
With Dad dispatched to the *workies*
Mam could work her alchemy.
It was a familiar mystery; each week
she charmed those crooked veg into elixir.
By the time Dad returned brimming
with beer and baccy, the house was awash
with scents of pork and gravy.
Together at the table we tucked into
plates piled high, a giant Yorkshire Pudding
like a clown's hat perched on top.
We ate till we could barely move
then begged for more.
Dad stole my pork; a secret gift
that silenced my meaty demons.

There was magic in those meals.
Later, when life had moved us
on to Sunday lunches far away,
the echo of Dad's *That was beautiful, pet*
as he squeezed Mam's hand
would remind us of those golden days.

A TRAIL OF TWO CITIES

                trailing between two cities   not here
nor there   not alone   nor unalone
everything the same   everything changed
no tongue   spent fleeting feelings
a palimpsest   of present   over past
                we pass
                the sunset gilded on municipal windows
hard as the gold of my ring
                a ring road by the Angel that never flies
                car headlights
tears stuck in eyes
                engines howl and hoot home
                our driver pauses then starts
like an almost-dead heart
                that's the pub where we talked about leaving
when the kids on this bus were in prams
                but only I went
and on and on
                the town between the cities
                salons a bleary glitter
                a stammering of stores
that will last as long as love   look up and above
you said   that's where the beauty is
all the time you knew
                the patchwork elephant outside the Indian restaurant
                fields stretch out their hands
that we would never last
                twilight wordlessly edging in
                a streetlamp showing an old man in neon
                smoking at a stand   I stand   thank the driver
                clamber down   back
not where I came from
                the place that is home
again
                for the first time   my son
                waits   into my arms
                to fly

WHEN THE SUN FELL OUT OF THE SKY

A dock leaf eases a sting
just as mint leaves soothe a tummy
ache. My mother taught me this,
just as hers taught her before.

My children know it will rain
when the cows in the field lie down.
They can smell the rain approaching.
I taught them that.

When the sun fell out of the sky
a rainbow appeared to staunch
the blue from bleeding. A shaft of sunlight
sent by Gaea was a gift of healing
splashing the world with pink.

NOTES ON THE POEMS

First Day for Liz

Elizabeth (Liz) Truss, the shortest-serving Prime Minister of the United Kingdom, became Prime Minister on 6th September 2022. Two days' later on 8th September, Elizabeth II, the longest-reigning British monarch, died.

First Day of Term

On 22nd August 2022, nine-year-old Olivia Pratt-Korbel was shot dead in Liverpool. The attack took place on her doorstep; the intended target was a gang member attempting to flee the gunman. Olivia was with her mother during the attack, the gunman's shot passing through her mother's wrist and into Olivia's chest.

ACKNOWLEDGEMENTS

'Night-light' is published by First Writer Magazine at https://www.firstwriter.com/competitions/poetry_competition/winners/12th poetry.shtml

'A Trail of Two Cities' is published by The Poetry Business in The North #68

'Skin' is published by Boats against the current poetry magazine

'First Day for Liz' is published by New Verse News.

www.ingramcontent.com/pod-product-compliance
Lightning Source LLC
Chambersburg PA
CBHW020141130526
44590CB00041B/634